INTERFACING EVANGELISM AND DISCIPLESHIP

Practical Evangelism and Discipleship Program

Instructional Guide

"Building the Kingdom with Intentional Evangelism and Discipleship of Souls"

Dr. Aaron R. Jones

INTERFACING EVANGELISM AND DISCIPLESHIP

Copyright © 2018 by Dr. Aaron R. Jones

Printed in the United States of America
Published by Kingdom Publishing, LLC, Odenton, Maryland

All rights reserved. No part of this book may be reproduced or transmitted in any form or by any means, electronic or mechanical, including photocopying, recording or by any information storage and retrieval system without written permission from the author, except for the inclusion of brief quotations in a review.

All scripture quotations are from the King James Version of the Bible. Thomas Nelson Publishers, Nashville: Thomas Nelson, Inc. 1972

Editor: Sharon D. Jones

Copyedited by Kimberly Curtis, Kingdom Publishing, LLC

Graphic Designer: Janell McIlwain (JM Virtual Concepts)

                Tiara Smith

ISBN: 978-1-947741-14-0

Library of Congress Control Number (LCCN): 2018947023

Table of Contents

Foreword .... - 1 -

Endorsements .... - 3 -

Preface .... - 10 -

Introduction and Philosophy .... - 14 -

5 Principles to Encourage Evangelism .... - 24 -

Components of Evangelism .... - 32 -

Bait for Evangelism .... - 40 -

Methodology of Evangelism .... - 46 -

Church Planting Produces Evangelism and Discipleship ..... - 58 -

Babes in Christ .... - 68 -

Components of Discipleship .... - 74 -

Evangelism and Discipleship Plan .... - 80 -

The Spirit of Forgiveness .... - 88 -

About the Author .... - 93 -

Works Cited .... - 96 -

Foreword

When God calls a man of faith and fortitude to a specific purpose in the building of His Kingdom, He uses an individual like Dr. Aaron Jones.

Feeling the urgency of the hour, Dr. Jones has shaped his participation in the FINISH Commitment by emphasizing the merging of evangelism and discipleship strategies to assist churches and individuals in their quests to effectively reach the lost. As Senior Pastor of New Hope Church of God, he is well-aware of what it takes to affect the Great Commission of our Lord.

Dr. Jones' desire is to instruct others on how to deliberately make an impact on winning souls and then discipling them for powerful Christian service. His all-inclusive approach will intrigue and provide the impetus for those willing to pursue the heart of God.

Interfacing Evangelism and Discipleship will change the course of your outreach!

Dr. Timothy M. Hill
General Overseer
Church of God, Cleveland, Tennessee

Endorsements

The supreme prerequisite of the church is soul winning, and discipleship; both are necessary for fulfilling the Great Commission. Isaiah 53 gives us Christ perspective on lost souls: "He poured out his life unto death, and was numbered with the transgressors. He bore the sin of many, and made intercession for the transgressors."

"Interfacing Evangelism and Discipleship" provides a robust, practical method for individuals and churches to return to the mandate delivered by Jesus Christ for making disciples of all people. Just as soldiers go through boot camp to learn how to use their weapons effectively, Dr. Jones takes us on a journey of hands-on involvement in evangelism and discipleship.

Bishop Steve Smith
Administrative Bishop, New York Church of God

"Dr. Aaron Jones has developed a tremendous resource offering practical application to the gospel movement tasks of evangelism and discipleship. This program bridges a significant gap between philosophical theory and theological practice providing the church with life changing tools to accomplish the great Commission."

Dr. Sean S. O'Neal, D.Min.
State Administrative Bishop, Arizona Church of God

Without question, the faith community finds itself challenged with deriving solutions that respond to the needs of both faith walkers and faith seekers. Daily, people find themselves bombarded with life disruption, constant discouragement, and nagging distractors. The cries for hope, faith, comfort and direction are poignant, and who is better positioned and equipped to answer these cries like the church can do, and I say this because as a body, the church has been divinely called to perform such good works in communities around the globe.

The Bible provides us with both the instruction and tools that those of us in ministry need to manifest action into results. The Bible offers us guidance as it relates to evangelism and discipleship, and it is for us, as Great Commission servant leaders, to commit ourselves intentionally to pursue this aspect of ministry.

Dr. Aaron R. Jones, a notable ministry servant leader in this book, "Interfacing Evangelism and Discipleship: Practical Evangelism and Discipleship

Endorsements

Program Instructional Manual" provides the reader with a roadmap, a capacity building toolkit that offers biblically based strategies and ministry approaches that can equip ministry teams in the establishment and elevation of their works in evangelism and discipleship. Dr. Jones details how to integrate Evangelism and Discipleship fully into a church's ministry work, as well as how to mesh the two effectively so that indeed the church is able to answer the cries of people from all walks of life who need the church like never before.
Peace and Divine Blessings,

Bishop Doyle P. Scott
Director, Church of God International Black Ministries Department

Interfacing Evangelism and Discipleship is cutting edge leadership material designed to empower the Body of Christ to accelerate. Dr. Jones' fresh ideas to engage in evangelism cause the reader to focus on a holistic approach that helps the believer to understand the challenges of building the Kingdom of God. His practical material provides holistic methodologies encapsulating the essence of equipping the saints to reap the harvest with passion, vision, wisdom, and care while closing the revolving back door and fostering relationships that establish continuity.

Kenneth L. Hill, D. Div.
Administrative Bishop
Church of God Southern New England

In an age of various technological advancement, the Church's assignment is still to "Go, Reach, and Teach." Dr. Jones has done a masterful job in mapping out a way for the body to do just that. This book is a great primer and should be part of every ministry's foundation.

Bishop Anthony T. Pelt
State Administrative Bishop
FL-Cocoa

In this practical ministry resource, Dr. Jones offers a roadmap that any church leader can use to build a system of evangelism and discipleship in their local church. I believe it's God's will that the local church become adept at administering these disciplines, and this work by Dr. Jones makes that possible. This resource will be easy to use and is ready-made for implementation. To say this work by Dr. Jones is timely is an understatement, especially in a world where the name of Jesus is often maligned and people are seeking answers. This is truly a powerful tool which

Endorsements

offers a structured approach to fulfilling the Great Commission. Invaluable!

Bishop James Izzard, Jr.
Senior Pastor, Life Builders Church of God
Forestville, MD

Dr. Aaron R. Jones' book, "Interfacing Evangelism and Discipleship" deals with the heart of God, winning the lost and making disciples of those that won to follow Jesus Christ. This book is simple and practical and provides the tools that are necessary for the training and development of young as well as seasoned believers in Christ. This is a must read for anyone who has a burden for the harvest of souls. This book is unique because of its combined approach of winning souls, "catching the fish" and discipling the convert, "cleaning the fish." This should be the top priority of every church today.

Dr. Aaron has lived out the contents of this book in his daily life and ministry that has impacted the New Hope Church of God where he is the Senior Pastor. The significant growth and development of that church is a direct result of the Lord Jesus using this young man and his wife as they lead the body of Christ in their area to a level of excellence in reaching lost souls for Jesus Christ. I strongly endorse this book and look forward to implementing this workbook in my local churches, here in New Jersey.

Bishop Dr. Philip M. Bonaparte
Senior Pastor, New Hope Church of God, New Jersey

"And he saith unto them, Follow me, and I will make you fishers of men."

MATTHEW 4:19

Preface

The call of the Church is to reach those who are lost to the Gospel of Jesus Christ. We are commanded to evangelize and disciple men and women. In the world that we live in today, this call is more vital than ever. The church must be more intentional about evangelism and discipleship. Many churches have vision statements or mission statements, but no evangelism or discipleship program to support it.

The church must prepare and train leaders and laity to reach the lost. The work of evangelism and discipleship is the heart of God. Since we know that God sent Jesus for the lost, why is the Church not allowing the winning and discipling of souls to be a priority? As the Church, we should not be satisfied until two things take place:

- All souls have been reached with the gospel of Jesus Christ and
- Souls have been discipled to grow in the name of the Lord.

Preface

Jesus birthed the mandate of evangelism and discipleship to His disciples (Matthew 4:19). Jesus called his disciples to leave their nets and become fishers of men. I believe the acts of fishermen involve evangelism and discipleship:

- Fishing for the fish is Evangelism.
- Cleaning the fish is Discipleship.

In the next ten sections, you will see how the Church can interface evangelism and discipleship to respond to the call. These sections will be providing information, insight, and inspiration toward evangelism and discipleship.

Relevant Questions

1.) Am I actively evangelizing my community?
_____
_____

2.) How many people am I presently discipling?
_____
_____

3.) How can I help my local church spread the Gospel?
_____
_____
_____

4.) Do I have an evangelism and discipleship program at my church?
_____
_____
_____

5.) When was the last time I led a person to Jesus Christ?
_____
_____
_____

"And he saith unto them, Follow me, and I will make you fishers of men."

MATTHEW 4:19

Introduction and Philosophy

The Objectives

Interfacing evangelism and discipleship will bring to life the importance of building the kingdom as commanded by God. The objectives of interfacing evangelism and discipleship are:

Objective #1—Ignite the Believer. The goal of this objective is to allow the Holy Spirit to light or re-ignite a fire in the believer. We must allow the Holy Spirit to work through us, so evangelism and discipleship can take place.

"But ye shall receive power, after that the Holy Ghost is come upon you: and ye shall be witnesses unto me both in Jerusalem, and in all Judaea, and in Samaria, and unto the uttermost part of the earth."
Acts 1:8

Objective #2--Inspire the Heart of the Believer. The goal of this objective is not only to inspire the believer, but through the Holy Spirit remain inspired. Souls saved and discipled should be the inspiration of every believer. Souls were the joy set before Jesus, that led Him to the cross.

~INSPIRE~

"Looking unto Jesus the author and finisher of our faith; who for the joy that was set before him endured the cross, despising the shame, and is set down at the right hand of the throne of God."
Hebrews 12:2

<u>Objective #3—Inform the Mind of the Believer</u>. The goal of this objective is to have the mind of Christ. The mind of Christ will keep us humble, compassionate, and focused on souls.

"Let this mind be in you, which was also in Christ Jesus."
Philippians 2:5

<u>Objective #4—Illuminate the Commandments of God</u>. The goal of this objective is to bring light to the scriptures that emphasize evangelism and discipleship.

Introduction and Philosophy

God's Word challenges us to have a lifestyle of evangelism and discipleship.

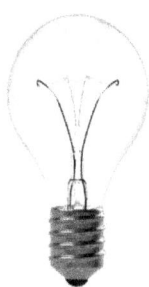

Illuminating Scriptures
- "The fruit of the righteous is a tree of life; and he that winneth souls is wise." (Proverbs 11:30)
- "Also I heard the voice of the Lord, saying, Whom shall I send, and who will go for us? Then said I, Here am I; send me. (Isaiah 6:8)
- "And in that day shall ye say, Praise the LORD, call upon his name, declare his doings among the people, make mention that his name is exalted." (Isaiah 12:4)
- "And Jesus came and spake unto them, saying, all power is given unto me in heaven and in earth." Go ye therefore, and teach all nations, baptizing them in the name of the Father, and of the Son, and of the Holy Ghost: Teaching them to observe all things whatsoever I have commanded you: and, lo, I am with you

always, even unto the end of the world. Amen." (Matthew 28:18-20)
- "And the things that thou hast heard of me among many witnesses, the same commit thou to faithful men, who shall be able to teach others also." (2 Timothy 2:2)
- "Then said Jesus to those Jews which believed on him, if ye continue in my word, then are ye my disciples indeed." (John 8:31)
- "Be ye followers of me, even as I also am of Christ. (1 Corinthians 11:1)
- "Let your light so shine before men, that they may see your good works, and glorify your Father which is in heaven. (Matthew 5:16)

Principles of Evangelism and Discipleship

Evangelism

Souls are the Heart of God.
"The Lord is not slack concerning his promise, as some men count slackness; but is longsuffering to us-ward, not willing that any should perish, but that all should come to repentance." (2 Peter 3:9)

"And I will put enmity between thee and the woman, and between thy seed and her seed; it shall bruise thy head, and thou shalt bruise his heel." (Genesis 3:15)

Introduction and Philosophy

The Redemption Plan for mankind began in Genesis 3:15. The plan was to reconcile mankind back to God. Yes, souls are the heartbeat of God. His longsuffering has allowed so many to experience His divine love.

Evangelism Teaches the Gospel
"Teaching them to observe all things whatsoever I have commanded you: and, lo, I am with you always, even unto the end of the world." (Matthew 28:20)

Evangelism is only about the Gospel of our Lord and Savior Jesus Christ. It is the center of Jesus' teachings. What makes evangelism so powerful is that it expresses the truth of Jesus' sacrifices on the cross.

A Tool Ordained by God
"Go ye therefore, and teach all nations, baptizing them in the name of the Father, and of the Son, and of the Holy Ghost." (Matthew 28:19)

The word that Jesus uses to activate this tool called evangelism is "GO". This is the word Jesus gave His disciples after His resurrection from the cross. Jesus wanted to ensure that the disciples understood that this is a very important tool.

Evangelism Leads Us to Christ

"For God so loved the world, that he gave his only begotten Son, that whosoever believeth in him should not perish, but have everlasting life." (John 3:16)

Evangelism is the direct path to Jesus. I love the words of the Savior in John 14:6 which says, "I am the way, the truth, and the life: no man cometh unto the Father, but by me." There is only one way to the Father and that is through Jesus. Evangelism is the road sign to The Way.

Evangelism Removes the Blinders

"In whom the god of this world hath blinded the minds of them which believe not, lest the light of the glorious gospel of Christ, who is the image of God, should shine unto them." (2 Corinthians 4:4)

The role and strategy of Satan is to keep blinders on unbelievers, so that the truth of Jesus is hidden. The Word must be spoken, so the blinders can be removed from the hearts and minds of the lost souls.

Discipleship

Discipleship is a Tool Ordained by God
"Teaching them to observe all things whatsoever I have commanded you: and, lo, I am with you always, even unto the end of the world." (Matthew 28:20)

Discipleship is a tool to give instruction, guidance, and wisdom. Discipleship is teaching others the life, character, and ministry of Jesus Christ.

Discipleship Establishes and Grows the Gospel in Us
"As newborn babes, desire the sincere milk of the word, that ye may grow thereby." (1 Peter 2:2)

The purpose of discipleship is so that maturity can take place in the life of the believer. Discipleship becomes the bridge between ignorance of the Word of God to obtaining knowledge of the Word of God.

Discipleship is for Those Found in Christ
"But as many as received him, to them gave he power to become the sons of God, even to them that believe on his name." (John 1:12)

No matter how successful you are in life, before you come to a saving knowledge of Jesus Christ, you are in sin. Discipleship is the defining element in the life of a believer to lead them in the right direction.

Discipleship Sharpens Our Vision
"Iron sharpeneth iron; so a man sharpeneth the countenance of his friend." (Proverbs 27:17)

If we are following the teachings and character of Jesus Christ, we will make other disciples. Discipleship helps to bring clarity to God's path for our lives and the church.

Discipleship Explains the Truth
"Sanctify them through thy truth: thy word is truth." (John 17:17)

Discipleship takes the new believers beyond their confession and acceptance of Jesus, as Lord and Savior of their life. Discipleship helps new believers understand their confession.

"And he saith unto them, Follow me, and I will make you fishers of men."

MATTHEW 4:19

5 Principles to Encourage Evangelism

The following principles should awaken the spirit-man in all believers. This awakening should cause believers to reach the lost at any cost. These 5 principles are meant to encourage and empower believers to evangelize.

Principle #1--The Last Day Mentality[i]

2 Timothy 3:1-5

"This know also, that in the last days perilous times shall come. For men shall be lovers of their own selves, covetous, boasters, proud, blasphemers, disobedient to parents, unthankful, unholy, without natural affection, trucebreakers, false accusers, incontinent, fierce, despisers of those that are good, Traitors, heady, highminded, lovers of pleasures more than lovers of God; Having a form of godliness, but denying the power thereof: from such turn away."

The last days are the times between Jesus' first coming and second coming. We are living in the crux of these times. Paul addresses the depravity mentality of man. Man's focus will center on self, pride, and materialism, not Jesus Christ. Paul's observation tells the church that evangelism is needed.

Principle #2—The Blood on Our Hands

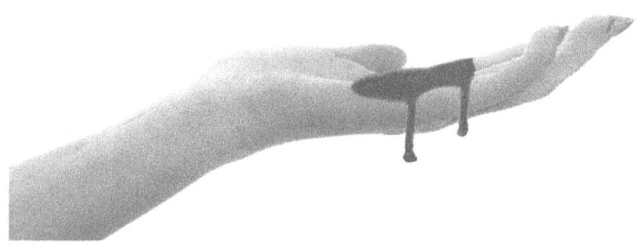

Ezekiel 3:17-19
"Son of man, I have made thee a watchman unto the house of Israel: therefore hear the word at my mouth, and give them warning from me. When I say unto the wicked, Thou shalt surely die; and thou givest him not warning, nor speakest to warn the wicked from his wicked way, to save his life; the same wicked man shall die in his iniquity; but his blood will I require at thine hand. "Yet if thou warn the wicked, and he turn not from his wickedness, nor from his wicked way, he shall die in his iniquity; but thou hast delivered thy soul."

Ezekiel gives us the watchman, the warning, and the wicked. God wants us to sound the alarm and warn people in relations to the gospel. God's Word is the warning message. God tells Ezekiel, if he warns the people, the blood will be released from his hand. But, if he doesn't, their blood belongs to him.

Principle #3—Desperate for One

Luke 15:3-7
"And he spake this parable unto them, saying, What man of you, having an hundred sheep, if he lose one of them, doth not leave the ninety and nine in the wilderness, and go after that which is lost, until he find it? And when he hath found it, he layeth it on his shoulders, rejoicing. And when he cometh home, he calleth together his friends and neighbours, saying unto them, Rejoice with me; for I have found my sheep which was lost. I say unto you, that likewise joy shall be in heaven over one sinner that repenteth, more than over ninety and nine just persons, which need no repentance."

The *"one"* is a very powerful concept for the kingdom. We must encourage the importance of the *"one."* The "*one*" may be a catalyst for multiplication. When we evangelize one, it may take us out of our comfort zone, but there is joy when that one comes into the kingdom.

Principle #4—The Harvest is Ready!

Matthew 9:37, 38
"Then saith he unto his disciples, "The harvest truly is plenteous, but the labourers are few; Pray ye therefore the Lord of the harvest, that he will send forth labourers into his harvest."

I believe the words of Christ were prophetic, even today, the harvest is plentiful but it remains to have few laborers.

Every believer is responsible for reaching the harvest. Keys to reaching the harvest: Help (Matthew 5:35,36), Love (Luke 19:10), Pray (Romans 10:1), Send (Acts 13:2), and Go (Isaiah 6:8).

Principle #5—Redeem the Time

Ephesians 5:15-16
"See then that ye walk circumspectly, not as fools, but as wise, redeeming the time, because the days are evil."

Today is the day you will witness to someone who doesn't know Jesus. No matter how many opportunities you missed, Redeem the Time now! There will always be doors of opportunity to share the good news.

"*And he saith unto them, Follow me, and I will make you fishers of men.*"
MATTHEW 4:19

Components of Evangelism

There are several components of evangelism. In this chapter, I will identify these components and how they work toward building the kingdom.

<u>The Mission</u>
The Great Commission (Matthew 28:18-20) is the mission of the Church. It should be the Churches centralized focus. A Church's success must be measured by the obedience and consistency to the Great Commission. All believers in the local church are called to evangelize. We are called to seek the unsaved and the

unchurched. This call must be through intentional efforts of the leaders and laity of the church.[ii]

The Commandment
The commandment to reach the lost is what we call Evangelism. Evangelism is simply spreading the good news of Jesus Christ. There will be times of pre-evangelism. Pre-evangelism is paving the way for Jesus. Through the Holy Spirit, we can prepare the way by finding common ground or removing obstacles of faith.

The Gospel
- ☐ God created us to be with Him.
- ☐ Our sin separated us from God.
- ☐ Sins cannot be removed by good deeds.
- ☐ Paying the price for sin, Jesus died and rose again.
- ☐ Everyone who trusts in Jesus alone has eternal life.
- ☐ Life eternal means we will be with Jesus forever.

The Requirement for Salvation (D.C.B.)
A Decision—to choose God over Satan

A Confession—that Jesus is Lord

A Belief—in the work of Jesus on the Cross

The Romans Road

A.P.L.S (All, Penalty, Love, and Salvation)

- Road #1—All Are Sinners and in Need of a Savior. (Romans 3:23)
- Road #2—The Penalty of Sin is Death.

(Romans 6:23)
- Road #3—Jesus' Expression of Love was to Die for our Sins. (Romans 5:8)
- Road #4—Salvation Comes Through a Confession and a Belief of Jesus' Work on the Cross. (Romans 10:9, 10)

The Heart of God, the Power of God, and the Increase of God

These 3 components identify God's approach to evangelism. God's heart beats for the unbelievers. He gives us the power to witness to the unbeliever, then He is responsible for adding the increase to the kingdom.[iii]

The Heart of God

II Peter 3:9
"The Lord is not slack concerning his promise, as some men count slackness; but is longsuffering to us-ward, not willing that any should perish, but that all should come to repentance."

I Timothy 2:4
"Who will have all men to be saved, and to come unto the knowledge of the truth."

The Power of God

Acts 1:8
"But ye shall receive power, after that the Holy Ghost is come upon you: and ye shall be witnesses unto me both in

Components of Evangelism

Jerusalem, and in all Judaea, and in Samaria, and unto the uttermost part of the earth."

The Increase of God

I Corinthians 3:6
"I have planted, Apollos watered; but God gave the increase."

The Facts About Evangelism[iv]

- No boundaries
- No respect of person
- Involves the teaching of the Gospel
- Must be led by the Holy Spirit
- Must be done in your community

- Brings repentance
- Involves preaching and teaching
- Limited to one message, but different methods
- Involves being active
- Involves a promise from Jesus Christ

Eight Keys to Evangelism[v]
- † Express Compassion (Jude 22)
- † Know to Listen (James 1:19)
- † Understand the Mindset of the Unbeliever (Romans 12:20)
- † Be Ready (I Peter 3:15)
- † Avoid Confrontation Conversation (Titus 3:9)
- † Observe Body Gestures and Countenances (Genesis 4:6)
- † Never Say "The Bible Says" Unless You Know and Can Quote the Scripture (II Timothy 2:15)
- † Adjust for Individuality (Genesis 1:26)

"*And he saith unto them, Follow me, and I will make you fishers of men.*"
MATTHEW 4:19

Bait for Evangelism

Fishers of Men

Jesus told His disciples, *"I will make you fishers of men (Matthew 4:19)."* How do we become fisher of men? First, we must allow God to be the Lord and Savior of our lives, then allow Him to guide our fishing path.

To Catch the Fish in the natural:

What type of type fish are you seeking?

What equipment is needed to catch the fish?

How deep is the water?

What bait will you use?
Where are the fish?

If we are going to be fishers of men, we must follow some of the principles in the natural. So, the question becomes, how do we translate the same principles into evangelism?

You will need the Holy Spirit to guide you through the following questions:

- ⊛ Who has God called you to?
- ⊛ What are you trying to reach?
- ⊛ What resources do you have?
- ⊛ What is the extent of the darkness?

Where is your Pond? Explain.

_____
_____
_____
_____
_____

The Gospel is the Believer's Net

Fishing Bait

- Is any substance used to attract and catch fish?
- What are you going to use to catch potential disciples?
- What will be the attraction tool?

Types of Bait
- Common Ground
- Love
- Breaking Bread
- Community Event
- Holy Spirit

When evangelism becomes a way of life, then fishing bait becomes a part of our daily thought process. You are thinking of ways to connect and introduce the gospel of Jesus Christ. Each person we approach may take different types of bait and this is where the Holy Spirit becomes crucial to evangelism.

"And he saith unto them, Follow me, and I will make you fishers of men."
MATTHEW 4:19

Methodology of Evangelism

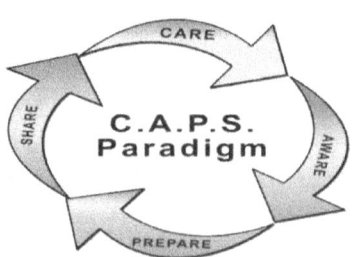

C.A.P.S. Paradigm (Care, Aware, Prepare, Share) is a methodology to evangelism that describes its scope from God's perspective and the individual believer. He wants the believers to examine their heart as it relates to the Great Commission and the words of Jesus. The C.A.P.S. Paradigm introduces only the Great Commission, but I believe the other great instructions from God as well. I describe this in Figure 1.

Figure 1

Care	The Great Call
Aware	The Great Command
Prepare	The Great Collection
Share	The Great Connection

The Great Commission

Jesus declares in Matthew 28:18-20,

"And Jesus came and spake unto them, saying, All power is given unto me in heaven and in earth. Go ye therefore, and teach all nations, baptizing them in the name of the Father, and of the Son, and of the Holy Ghost: Teaching them to observe all things whatsoever I have commanded you: and, lo, I am with you always, even unto the end of the world. Amen."

This commission should be known to every believer. Jesus is challenging the Church to fulfill its divine call and the very reason for its existence. It is not just a good slogan or spiritual words; it is the mission of the Church.

_____
_____
_____

Methodology #1
CARE
The Great Call

Matthew 25:35,36
APPROACH

Thirsty • Hungry • Stranger • Prison • Naked

Unbeliever
Lost Soul
Person

C A R E

"For I was an hungred, and ye gave me meat: I was thirsty, and ye gave me drink: I was a stranger, and ye took me in: Naked, and ye clothed me: I was sick, and ye visited me: I was in prison, and ye came unto me."

Evangelism is about reaching the needs of people. We operate as true children of God when we spread the love of God. Meeting people's needs has a way of opening the doors of their heart. If you want people to hear what you have to say about Jesus, show them what you see about their need. Jesus says, when we do for others, we are doing for Him (Matthew 25:45).

There are many needs in the world, but Jesus saw fit to identify those who are hungry, thirsty, naked, and need to be visited.

Methodology #2
AWARE
The Great Command

> *"But ye shall receive power, after that the Holy Ghost is come upon you: and ye shall be witnesses unto me both in Jerusalem, and in all Judaea, and in Samaria, and unto the uttermost part of the earth."*
> (Acts 1:8)

Jesus prophecies to His disciples about the coming power that will assist them in the fulfillment of God's divine plan for evangelism. Jesus lets the disciples know that the Holy Spirit will possess them in a supernatural way. The Holy Spirit will give them power so they can be witnesses. Jesus gives a path or outline on how the gospel will spread.

Where is your Jerusalem?
_____
_____

Where is your Judea and Samaria?
_____
_____

Where is your uttermost part of the earth?
_____
_____

Acts 1:8 lets us know there are no boundaries to spreading the gospel.
___
___

Where is God calling you on the triangle?
___
___

Methodology #3
Prepare

The Great Collection

"But the fruit of the Spirit is love, joy, peace, longsuffering, gentleness, goodness, faith, Meekness, temperance: against such there is no law."

Allow God to prepare your heart and pray daily for a heart towards souls. Operating by the fruit of the Spirit is crucial to evangelism. We must live a lifestyle of walking in love, joy, peace, longsuffering, gentleness, goodness, and faith. The nature of fruit is to reproduce itself, provide strength, and be appealing to the eye.

Methodology #4
Share
John 4:28, 29

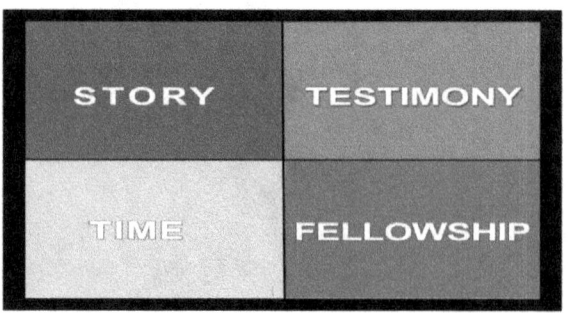

SHARE

"The woman then left her waterpot, and went her way into the city, and saith to the men, Come, see a man, which told me all things that ever I did: is not this the Christ."

<u>Story</u>—Everyone has a story to tell. Your transparency opens doors of the unbeliever's heart.

- What is your story?

_____
_____
_____
_____
_____

<u>Testimony</u>—What darkness did God remove from your life?

- What is testimony?

_____
_____
_____
_____
_____

Time
- How much time are you willing to give up for a lost soul?

_____

_____

_____

Fellowship—One meal may make a world of difference. Jesus engaged with the unbeliever, but did not conform to the world.

The Two by Two Rule

"And he called unto him the twelve, and began to send them forth by two and two, and gave them power over unclean spirit."
Mark 6:7

Why go out two by two?

- To have a witness
- To have one person praying
- To provide protection
- To establish connection

Types of Evangelism

There are various ways we can present the gospel to evangelize and reach souls for the kingdom of God.

How can you, your church, or your ministry utilize the following approaches to build the kingdom of God?

- Church Planting
- Street (Corner, Door-to Door)
- Outreach (Nursing/Hospital, Prison, Clothing, and Food Pantry)
- Small Groups
- Personal (Job, Home)
- Mall
- Prayer Wash

_____
_____
_____
_____
_____
_____

"And he saith unto them, Follow me, and I will make you fishers of men."
MATTHEW 4:19

Church Planting Produces Evangelism and Discipleship

The nature of church planting opens doors for evangelism and discipleship across the world. Each church has its own culture and is able to reach certain groups of people. It has been said that the survival of the Church in many ways is dependent on church planting. The Apostle Paul was a church planter; he planted churches as a way to spread the Gospel of Jesus Christ.

One reason why church plants are important is because they have the opportunity to bring new energy, new connections, and new vision to a community. Evangelism and discipleship should be the focus of all church plants.

<u>6 Statistics Every Church Planter Needs to Know</u>[vi]
- Less than 18% of Americans attend church!
- There are 156 million unchurched in the US
- 47% of America's unchurched is open to being invited to church by a friend
- Churches that plant, grow three times faster
- A new church gains 60-80% of its membership from new conversion

Myths of Church Planting

Church planting is a kingdom expansion method that we find in scriptures. When church planting is inspired by God, it will be a key element for evangelism and discipleship. Many church leaders are discouraged from church planting because of the known myths of church planting. It would be a powerful tool, if every pastor could embrace the idea of church planting.

1. Myth #1: Church planting will hinder the growth of other churches.
2. Myth #2: There are already enough churches in our community.
3. Myth #3: Church planting is not a successful tool for growth in the body of Christ.
4. Myth #4: Our church cannot support a church plant.
5. Myth #5: Church planting creates division in the body of Christ.
6. Myth #6: Church planting makes existing church's irrelevant.

Basic Church Plant Components

Church planting is a calling from God. When God calls a church planter, He will see that all needs will be met. It takes complete trust in God, in His plan, and in His path. Proverbs 3:5, 6 says, *"Trust in the LORD with all thine heart; and lean not unto thine own understanding. In all thy ways acknowledge him, and he shall direct thy paths."*

Below are different components every church planter must not only consider, but see that it becomes a part of his DNA:

- Know your calling
- Know your community
- Conduct a Demographical Study
- Identify the Vision
- Identify the Purpose
- Know your Core Values.
- Have an Outreach Plan
- Connect with partners/supporters/community leaders/local schools
- Recruit a Launch Team
- Develop a Timeline
- Create a Budget

Bi-Vocational Dynamic

- It has been said that two-thirds of churches in America are pastored by bi-vocational pastors.

- Also, Only 7% of pastors in Protestant churches are between the ages of 28–45.

Oftentimes, new church plants are done by pastors who have a full-time or part-time job. There are benefits to being a Bi-Vocational Pastor, whether planting a new church or assuming a church.

Benefits of a Bi-Vocational Pastor[vii]

⊛ There is usually a stronger financial base for both the pastor and the church

Church Planting Produces Evangelism and Discipleship

- ⊛ A Stronger financial base allows the ministry to do more outreach and missions

- ⊛ Pastors can lead with more freedom, because they are less afraid of obstinate leaders. Obstinate leaders don't threaten his/her complete livelihood.

- ⊛ They tend to engage more laypersons in ministry—out of necessity.

- ⊛ Congregation adjusts its expectations—they don't expect a superman or superwoman.

- ⊛ They may be more in touch with everyday challenges of a person who works and faces the trials of vocation.

- ⊛ They stay fresh in their ability to engage in personal evangelism (at work).

- ⊛ They tend to maximize time because they have to do more with less time.

G.R.A.C.E.[viii]

G.R.A.C.E. is an acrostic to encourage bi-vocational pastors and church planters

† G—God

† R—Relationship

† A—Affirmation

† C—Care

† E—Expectation

† Always keep **God** as the focus—not ministry.

† Intentionally cultivate your personal **relationship** with Christ.

† Learn to affirm yourself and accept **affirmation** from those closest to you.

† You MUST practice **self-care**.

† Adjust your **expectations**.

Developing the Team

Questions to Ask

- What is the make-up of a good team?
    - Children's Leader
    - Worship Leader

Church Planting Produces Evangelism and Discipleship

- First Impressions Leader
- Administrative Support/Leader

■ What should be the DNA of a good team?

The DNA (Acts 6:3)[ix]
- **Integrity**—Your team members must be people who demonstrate high integrity.

- **Spiritual**—Your team members must be spiritual.

- **Competent**—Your team members must be competent.

- **Committed**—Your team members must be committed

■ How do you mobilize your team? How do you help them become effective?

How to Mobilize a Team
† Train Them
† Empower Them
† Release Them

"And he saith unto them, Follow me, and I will make you fishers of men."
MATTHEW 4:19

Interfacing Evangelism and Discipleship

Babes in Christ

1 Peter 2:2 Paradigm

"As newborn babes, desire the sincere milk of the word, that ye may grow thereby:"

- A new believer is a babe in Christ. The age of conversion doesn't determine the growth.
- The Greek word for "babe" is *nepious,*
    - Infant
    - Little child

- Untaught
- Unskilled

Understanding the Babe in Christ

When we are born again, we become spiritual newborn babies (John 3:1-8). The need for milk is a natural instinct for a baby, and it signals the desire for nourishment that will lead to growth. Once we see our need for God's Word and begin to find nourishment in Christ, our spiritual appetite will increase. We will begin to mature. You need the milk of the Word of God. The Father's food is the Word of God. Children tend to grow up and want to do as adults. Babes in Christ want to grow up to be like Jesus.

The Benefits of Milk

What is Milk? Milk contains all the nutrient substances to help the physical body to grow and be strong. God's Word has all the necessary nutrients to help the babe in Christ grow and be strong. There must be continual pray that one's appetite for God's Word grows daily.

Babes in Christ Experience the New

■ New Creature

"*Therefore if any man be in Christ, he is a <u>new creature</u>: old things are passed away; behold all things become new.*"

II Corinthians 5:17

■ New Family Relationships

"*Now therefore ye are no more strangers and foreigners, <u>but fellow citizens with the saints</u>, and of the household of God.*"

Ephesians 2:19

- ■   New Eternal Home

"*For we know that if our earthly house of this tabernacle were dissolved, <u>we have a building of God</u>, a house not made with hands, eternal in the heavens.*"

2 Corinthians 5:1

- ■   New Inheritance (Romans 8:17)

"*And if children, heirs also, heirs of God and fellow heirs with Christ, if indeed we suffer with Him so that we may also be glorified with Him.*"

Romans 8:17

"And he saith unto them, Follow me, and I will make you fishers of men."
MATTHEW 4:19

Components of Discipleship

What is Christian Discipleship?

Christian discipleship accepts the words and workings of Jesus Christ. It involves training believers on how to apply His words and workings.

Characteristics of a Disciple

- D—Desires the presence of God

- I—Ignites others around them by the Holy Spirit

- S—Stands in prayer for the church, his family, and the world

- C—Concerned about God's Kingdom

- I—Involves oneself in outreach

- P—Plans daily devotional time with God

- L—Leaves the sinful past behind

- E—Exemplifies the teachings of Jesus

7 Conclusions to Discipleship[x]

Every day the world is creating disciples. The world uses things that feel good to draw disciples, regardless of the consequences. The world presents a powerful influence. As believers, we are called to be followers, but not followers of this world.

† A disciple of Jesus understands the command of God, the challenge from God, and the changed lifestyle for God.

† As disciples and soldiers of Jesus Christ, we have a great assignment. Our assignment is to help

others to see that the destruction of eternal lives is at stake.

Conclusion #1—Jesus Must Be the #1 Priority
"If any man come to me, and hate not his father, and mother, and wife, and children, and brethren, and sisters, yea, and his own life also, he cannot be my disciple."
Luke 14:26

Conclusion #2—Must Stay on the Path (Journey)
"And whosoever doth not bear his cross, and come after me cannot be my disciple."
Luke 14:27

Conclusion #3—Must Count the Price (Cost)
"For which of you, intending to build a tower, sitteth not down first, and counteth the cost, whether he have sufficient to finish it?"
Luke 14:28

Conclusion #4—Must Not Cling to Earthly Possessions
"So likewise, whosoever he be of you that forsaketh not all that he hath, he cannot by my disciple."
Luke 14:33

Components of Discipleship

Conclusion #5—Must Be Productive
"Herein is my Father glorified, that ye bear much fruit; so shall ye be my disciples."

John 15:8

Conclusion #6—Must Have Passion
"By this shall all men know that ye are my disciple, if ye have love one to another."

John 13:35

Conclusion #7—Must Know His Position
"The disciple is not above his master, nor the servant above his lord."

Matthew 10:24

"And he saith unto them, Follow me, and I will make you fishers of men."

MATTHEW 4:19

Evangelism and Discipleship Plan

Leadership' Role in Evangelism and Discipleship

Leadership's involvement in evangelism and discipleship is very important. Leadership's engagement can be an agent of success or challenge as it pertains to evangelism and discipleship. Leadership must have an intentional and identified role in order to have the greatest impact for growth.

LEADERSHIP'S ROLE IS:

To Provide Vision
"Where there is no vision, the people perish: but he that keepeth the law, happy is he."
Proverbs 29:18

- What is your vision for Evangelism?

_____
_____
_____
_____

- What is your vision for Discipleship?

_____
_____
_____

To Provide Resources
"He saith unto them, How many loaves have ye? go and see. And when they knew, they say, Five, and two fishes."
Mark 6:38

- What do you have?

  _____
  _____
  _____
  _____

- What is your budget?

  _____
  _____
  _____
  _____

- How will you raise funds or receive donations?

  _____
  _____
  _____
  _____

To Provide a Manual

"And the Lord answered me, and said, Write the vision, and make it plain upon tables, that he may run that readeth it."

Habakkuk 2:2

- What are the policies and procedures?

  _____
  _____

- Who can develop the manual?

_____
_____
_____
_____
_____

To Provide Intentionality

"For I know the thoughts that I think toward you, saith the Lord, thoughts of peace, and not of evil, to give you an expected end."

Jeremiah 29:11

- How intentional are you about building God's Kingdom?

_____
_____
_____
_____

- What are your steps of intention?

_____
_____

To Provide an Example
"Be ye followers of me, even as I also am of Christ."
I Corinthians 11:1

- Jesus was the example of Evangelism and Discipleship.

- A title or position doesn't remove the responsibility of evangelizing and discipling.

- Evangelism and discipleship may take different forms as you move in ministry.

To Provide Training
"But the Comforter, which is the Holy Ghost, whom the Father will send in my name, he shall teach you all things, and bring all things to your remembrance, whatsoever I have said unto you."
John 14:26

- Jesus trained His disciples.

- Training provides a continuum of evangelism and discipleship

2 Timothy 2:2 Approach

"And the things that thou hast heard of me among many witnesses, the same commit thou to faithful men, who shall be able to teach others also."

The Apostle Paul mentoring Timothy is what I view as the focused approaches to discipleship.

- The Recollection

"And the <u>things that thou hast heard of me</u> among many witnesses…"

- The Release

"…the same <u>commit thou</u> to faithful men…"

Interfacing Evangelism and Discipleship

- ## The Reproduction

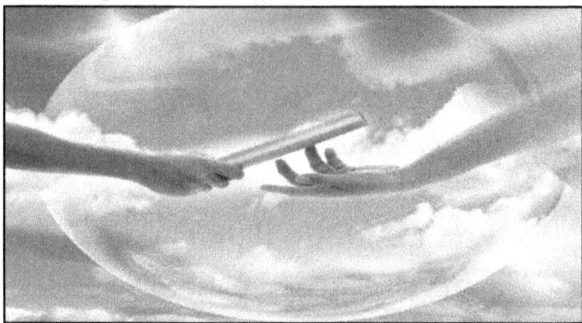

"...who shall be able to <u>teach others</u> also."

"And he saith unto them, Follow me, and I will make you fishers of men."
MATTHEW 4:19

The Spirit of Forgiveness

Our forgiveness should be the drive to fulfill the call to Evangelism and Discipleship. The love of God produced such a power of intervention to our sins. God sending Jesus became the center of our sins being removed from our lives.

God's Power of Forgiveness

The power of God's forgiveness is shown in scripture:
- Doesn't Remember (Isaiah 43:25)
- East to West disposal (Psalm 103:12)

- Sea Bound (Micah 7:20)

The Importance of Forgiveness

- The reason why we are able to forgive is because we were forgiven of all our sins.
- Evangelism and discipleship become easier when we carry a heart of forgiveness.
- Our approach to people must be in the spirit of forgiveness.
- Lack of forgiveness interferes with our relationship with God.
  - Matthew 6:15— <u>*"But if ye forgive not men their trespasses, neither will your Father forgive your trespasses."*</u>

Scriptural Support for Forgiveness

- *"For if ye forgive men their trespasses, your heavenly Father will also forgive you."* (Matthew 6:14)
- *"And be ye kind one to another, tenderhearted, forgiving one another, even as God for Christ's sake hath forgiven you."* (Ephesians 4:32)
- *"Then came Peter to him, and said, Lord, how oft shall my brother sin against me, and I forgive him? till seven times? Jesus saith unto him, I say not unto thee, Until seven times: but, Until seventy times seven."* (Matthew 18:21, 22)

- *"Forbearing one another, and forgiving one another, if any man have a quarrel against any: even as Christ forgave you, so also do ye."* (Colossians 3:13)

A.C.T.

"He that covereth his sins shall not prosper: but whoso confesseth and forsaketh them shall have mercy."
Proverbs 28:13

Forgiveness is an A.C.T.[xi]

- Admission
- Confession
- Transformation

<u>Admission</u>

<u>*"He that covereth his sins shall not prosper…"*</u>

- Refuse to cover the sin of unforgiveness any longer
- We must admit and realize there is a problem.

- Without admission we will continue to walk in unforgiveness.

- Forgiveness cannot take place without God

Confession

"...but whoso confesseth..."

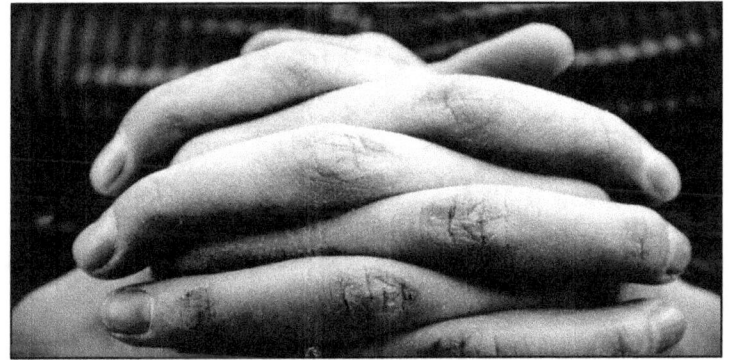

- Confession is the path to forgiveness. (1John 1:9)

- Confession is the path to being cleansed. (1 John 1:9)

- Confession is the path to righteousness. (1 John 1:9)

- Confession is the path to healing. (James 5:16)

Transformation

"...forsaketh them shall have mercy."

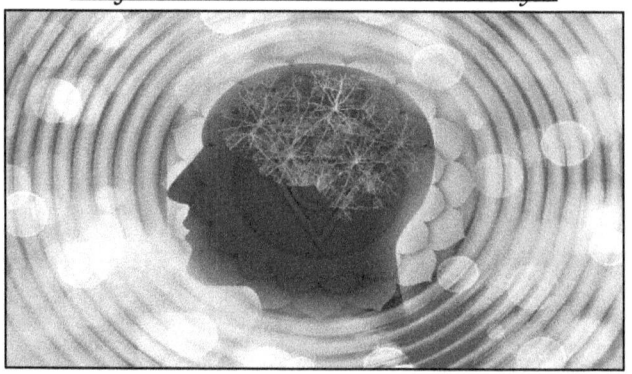

- I must change!
- "forsake"—abandon and be transformed
- Romans 12:2—renewing the mind
- Transformation takes place when there is a change of heart by the power of God.

About the Author

Dr. Aaron R. Jones serves as Senior Pastor of New Hope Church of God. Under his pastorate is New Hope Kiddie Kollege, Inc (Daycare) and New Hope Community Outreach Services, Inc. Dr. Jones also oversees New Hope Church of God Ghana (2 churches) and New Hope Church of God Uganda (3 churches).

Dr. Jones is an Ordained Bishop with the Church of God denomination and is the DELMARVA-DC

District Overseer (16 churches). Dr. Jones serves on DELMARVA-DC's Regional Council, Ministerial Internship Program Board, Urban Ministry Committee, Finance Committee, and Chaplain's Board. He also serves on both the Church of God's International and DELMARVA-DC Ministry to the Military Board. In his local community, Dr. Jones serves as a Chaplain for the Charles County Sheriff Department. He also serves as Board Secretary for the United Ministers Coalition of Southern Maryland, Inc.

Being obedient to 2 Timothy 2:15, "Study to show thyself approved...," Dr. Jones received a Doctorate in Theology and Pastoral Counseling from Life Christian University and a Doctorate in Christian Counseling from American Christian College and Seminary. He is a certified Pastoral Counselor with the International Association of Christian Counseling Professionals. He is a Life and Pastoral Coach. He is the former Executive Vice President of the National Bible College and Seminary in Fort Washington, Maryland.

Dr. Jones has published ten books and a soul-wininng project that provide a biblical foundation for Christian doctrine and discipline. He has recorded a CD entitled, Peace in the Storm. He is the founder and owner of God's Comfort Ministries, LLC, which provides Christian literature, evangelism training, and spiritual guidance. He has appeared live on TCT

About the Author

Network; WATC-TV's Atlanta Live; Babbie's House (hosted by CCM artist Babbie Mason); and In Concert Today on DCTV. He has done radio interviews with Radio One's WYCB's program; The Praise Fest Show; and online with Total Prayze. He was featured on the cover of Change Gospel Magazine and interviewed on Promoting Purpose Magazine.

Dr. Jones not only serves God, but his country as well. He has served over 20 years in the Armed Forces. He is a retired Chaplain with the Army National Guard. He participated in both Operation Noble Eagle (2003) and Operation Iraqi Freedom III (2005).

Dr. Jones is happily married to the former Sharon Russell. He sincerely believes without her love, support, and encouragement, many of his goals would not have been accomplished.

Works Cited

[i] Jones, Aaron R., The Soul Initiative for Eternity. (Denton: Kingdom Kaught Publishing, LLC), 2015.

[ii] Jones, Aaron R., Equipping the Church for the Harvest. (Cheltenham: Anointed Press Publishing), 2009.

[iii] Jones, Aaron R., Equipping the Church for the Harvest. (Cheltenham: Anointed Press Publishing), 2009.

[iv] Jones, Aaron R., Equipping the Church for the Harvest. (Cheltenham: Anointed Press Publishing), 2009.

[v] Jones, Aaron R., Eight Effective Keys to Evangelism. (Cheltenham: Anointed Press Publishing), 2003.

[vi] "6 Statistics Every Church Planter Needs to Know," Portable Church, 2016, www.portablechurch.com/2016/06/

[vii] Izzard, James, GRACE for the Tentmaker-Manuscript. (Upper Marlboro, Maryland), 2017.

[viii] Izzard, James, GRACE for the Tentmaker-Manuscript. (Upper Marlboro, Maryland), 2017.

[ix] Izzard, James, GRACE for the Tentmaker-Manuscript. (Upper Marlboro, Maryland), 2017.

[x] Jones, Aaron R., The Disciple's Conclusion. (Denton: Kingdom Kaught Publishing, LLC), 2015.

[xi] Bonaparte, Philip and Solomon, Wayne. Forgiveness from the Heart (Clermont: S & B Publications), 2017.

www.ingramcontent.com/pod-product-compliance
Lightning Source LLC
Chambersburg PA
CBHW071532080526
44588CB00011B/1650